☙

Welcome to your Walking Stick Press guided
journal. Within these pages you'll find:

☙

instruction to guide you on your way

☙

writing prompts to lead you to your goal

☙

space to record your responses to the prompts—to
map your insights as you heal, grow and explore

☙

Along the way, feel free to jot in the margins,
add your own quotes,
let writing take you down a trail you didn't expect.
Enjoy the journey.

☙

The Book
of
Self-Acquaintance

ഔ

a guided journal

Margaret Tiberio

Walking Stick Press

Cincinnati, Ohio

∾

Visit our Web site at www.writersdigest.com for information on more resources for writers.

To receive a free weekly E-mail newsletter delivering tips and updates about writing and about Writer's Digest products, send an E-mail with "Subscribe Newsletter" in the body of the message to: newsletter-request@writersdigest.com, or register directly at our Web site at www.writersdigest.com.

05 04 03 02 01   5 4 3 2 1

Library of Congress Cataloging in Publication Data

Tiberio, Margaret.
    The book of self-acquaintance: a guided journal / by Margaret Tiberio
        p.   cm.
    ISBN 1-58297-022-X (alk. paper)
    1. Self-perception 2. Self-evaluation. 3. Introspection. 4. Diaries--Authorship. I. Title.
BF697.5.S43 T53 2000   00-043487
158.1--dc21   CIP

Edited by Jack Heffron, Meg Leder and Jessica Yerega
Cover and interior design by Matthew S. Gaynor
Production coordinated by Mark Griffin
Photographs by Margaret Tiberio

Dedication

For my parents.

About the Author

Margaret Tiberio wrote this book while developing
an autobiographical curriculum for a school-based
counseling program in Boston. She has worked
for social service agencies in Great Britain and
Massachusetts and in public television at WGBH-
TV. A social worker since 1980, she has consistently
used journal writing as a therapeutic tool for adults
and children. She regularly conducts photography
workshops and is currently an advocate at a battered
women's program in Salem, Massachusetts.

Table of Contents

Introduction *page 1*

Chapter 1 **My Self** *page 6*

Chapter 2 **My Body** *page 28*

Chapter 3 **Myself With Others** *page 40*

Chapter 4 **Myself Alone** *page 66*

Chapter 5 **Myself in Time** *page 84*

Chapter 6 **Myself in the World** *page 96*

Chapter 7 **Myself in Nature** *page 108*

Chapter 8 **My Life Course** *page 122*

❧

Introduction

> It is not easy to know what you like.
> Most people fool themselves their en-
> tire lives through about this. Self-
> Acquaintance is a rare condition.
>
> Robert Henri
>
> *The Art Spirit*

W hen painter and teacher Robert Henri asserts "it is not easy to know what you like," I believe he's writing about the importance of preferences in creating art and making a life. A true preference is not necessarily a superficial matter, because it is how we define and practice, when faced with choices, who we are in the world. Some of our preferences make themselves known when we are very young; others surface unexpectedly in later years. As we become conscious of them, we recognize these practices as innate, related to an essential part of ourselves. Whatever we are strongly drawn to represents a link to our deepest and perhaps most original qualities. So, to find out *what we like*—in other people, in the natural world, in our work, anywhere at any time—is to approach an understanding of who we are and who we may become.

Henri uses the term *self-acquaintance*, not *self-knowledge*, which I believe is deliberate. Rather than the claim of expertise implied by the word *knowledge*—a summing up of what is known—*acquaintance* is a lighter word, meaning familiarity, with the possibility of surprise and openness—an acknowledgement that there is more to be known and experienced.

Henri also writes, "artists are people who use what they have." To engage in autobiographical work is to do what artists do: to use life experience to observe, collect, select and elaborate. We begin with what we know about ourselves—our preferences, our temperament, the time and place in which we live—and, like an artist, represent what is meaningful. Reading the autobiographical work of great writers has taught me a valuable lesson: we all *write* our own lives according to what we turn our attention to, what we remember and how we recollect.

I began this book as a counselor based in the Boston Public Schools, working to develop an autobiographical curriculum that would teach students how to tell their own stories through writing and photography. The curriculum was created for children who were experiencing upheaval in their lives—through recent immigration, a serious illness or death in the family, or having been a witness to a violent act in the community or in their own homes. We began by asking students direct questions about their preferences, their observations and important life events. As we had hoped, the process was a pleasurable and sometimes therapeutic one; the students became less overwhelmed and more hopeful, absorbed in the task of describing who they were and what they knew.

The simple questions posed to those schoolchildren became the foundation for this book. Our lives are abundant with observations and events that have meaning for us—that when closely examined reveal to us who we are and what we truly value. We need to take the time to ask key questions so that the answers, in the form of specific details, can come readily to mind. This book was written with respect for the definitive power of words. Finding the precise word or phrase can clarify experiences that have been only partially understood. I hope that the questions and expressions in each chapter will also act as prompts to highlight dimly held thoughts and memories. Specific episodes in our lives can be examined again and again in the light of the new evidence of the present. Circumstances in the present will always influence how we view the past. Our memories comprise our relationship to the past, but they are fluid and subject to change, often having the peculiar logic and power of dreams. If memories are the stuff our lives are made of, we should feel free to work with them consciously and creatively.

I decided to create a workbook for autobiographical writing for those of us who would like to work in a journal but have found it difficult to begin or sustain our efforts. I recognize that most of us have little time for reflection and would appreciate a book with directed questions that we can open and soon begin writing in. The book was also designed for writers at any stage of composing a memoir and for artists in any discipline whose work is expressly autobiographical. If you're a fiction writer, you may find the following chapters useful in developing the material for your characters' stories. If you're a therapist, I also want to recommend this book for the benefit of your clients. Writing can allow for more privacy and focus than conversation. Within silence and in a slower tempo, other insights and ideas may be expressed.

While exploring this book, feel free to move in any direction you like. I urge you to begin with the pages you feel drawn to, passing over any sections that are less appealing. There is no need to be either thorough *or* concise. There is no special benefit in completing every question in each chapter, nor is there any limit to how much you can write for each question. The simple purpose is to allow you to use any form of descriptive writing—lists of words, sentence fragments, prose or poetry—to record the elements of your life history.

We *recall, remember, recollect, recount* and *retrieve* our memories. When we use these words in relation to storytelling, specifically the telling of our own stories, they indicate a concentrated effort, undertaken again and again. We construct our lives through our actions and decisions, but also in the act of telling. More than we may know, we shape the circumstances of our lives into stories. In the face of good fortune or misfortune, there is a great need to find our place in the story and find a meaning we can live with. We need intellect and imagination to make sense of what has happened throughout our lives. There is no reason to accept that the last word has been said on our life story. With storytelling, we can always start at the beginning. When we tell stories, we reveal what was really at stake, while seeking to find the balance of human intention and fate. To suffuse events with an understanding and emphasis that we have pieced together ourselves is to invite meaning and dignity into our lives.

When we describe what our lives have been and meant, we enlarge our sense of who we are today. Events in the present take on a new significance as we acknowledge that aspects of ourselves are worthy of close attention. In giving us the opportunity to pay homage to the details of our lives, autobiographical work is inherently linked to what we call the will to live. Self-acquaintance may be, as Robert Henri has written, a rare condition, but it may also be the key to living wholeheartedly.

1
My Self

Be yourself today, don't wait until tomorrow. He who is master of what he has today, will be master of what he has tomorrow. Many things we know are true we have never made a part of us...masters are people who use what they have.

Robert Henri
The Art Spirit

I am the child of _____

_____

Born on_____

_____

At_____

_____

I was named for_____

_____

What is the meaning of my name?_____

_____

What is the origin of my name?_____

_____

This is the first home I can remember_____

_____

Who else was living there?_____

_____

The natural environment of my birthplace could be described as_____

_____

I would describe the social environment of my birthplace as_____

_____

Who cared for me when I was young?_____

_____

These are my earliest memories_____

_____

8 | Who were my childhood companions?_____

_____

Where did we play?_____

_____

What did we do there?_____

_____

What did I see on my way to school?_____

_____

Do I remember learning to read?_____

_____

How did I find my place in school during the earliest years? _____

_____

As a child I...

was given_____

_____

was afraid to ask for_____

_____

was inconsolable when_____

_____

was responsible for_____

_____

always knew_____

_____

felt safe when_____

_____

felt loved by_____

_____

could spend hours_____

_____

was told I was_____

_____

was called_____

_____

was forbidden to_____

_____

was indulged when_____

_____

was expected to_____

_____

was encouraged to_____

_____

had a great appetite for_____

_____

was bored by_____

_____

always sensed that_____

_____

10 | As a child I...

overheard_____

_____

lived in dread of_____

_____

never knew why_____

_____

had a natural ability for_____

_____

was praised for_____

_____

lived in the shadow of_____

_____

outshone_____

_____

was caught_____

_____

was fascinated by_____

_____

loved the taste of_____

_____

loved to wear_____

_____

wanted to become like_____

_____

swore I never would_____

_____

was confused by_____

_____

was cranky when_____

_____

was beside myself with joy when_____

_____

was nurtured by_____

_____

imagined_____

_____

imagined as real_____

_____

Features of my childhood that come to mind strongly...

memorable gifts_____

_____

recurring nightmares_____

_____

favorite games_____

_____

12 | Features of my childhood that come to mind strongly...

impossible wishes_____

_____

family dramas_____

_____

intrusions from the outside world_____

_____

shining moments_____

_____

My life story as told by a sympathetic third party...

"The first thing you should know_____

_____

"When she was born_____

_____

"Her mother_____

_____

"Her father_____

_____

"As a child she_____

_____

"As a young woman she_____

_____

"She met_____

_____

"She learned_____

_____

"She feared_____

_____

"She overcame_____

_____

"She was wounded by_____

_____

"She always enjoyed_____

_____

"Due to her family circumstances, she_____

_____

"She had a real talent for_____

_____

"She was knowledgeable about_____

_____

"She was well loved by_____

_____

"She surprised us all when_____

_____

"She was never happier than when she_____

_____

"I wish she could have known that_____

_____

14 | My life story as told by a sympathetic third party...

"One day she was discovered_____

_____

"Her greatest challenge was_____

_____

"She gave birth to_____

_____

"I saw a change in her when_____

_____

"She mastered the art of_____

_____

"She had a true gift for_____

_____

"And so she_____

_____

"And then she_____

_____

"And ultimately she_____

_____

Where do I go for information about myself?_____

_____

What words have I used to define myself?_____

_____

What words have been used by others to describe me?_____

_____

What do the words really mean?_____

_____

What do I agree to be true?_____

_____

What do I hope to be true?_____

_____

What do I reject?_____

_____

It seems that this is the hand I have been dealt with regard to...

    money_____

_____

    health_____

_____

    abilities_____

_____

    obstacles_____

_____

    good fortune_____

_____

    love_____

_____

If I could, would I change...

    my name?_____

_____

16 | If I could, would I change...

my race?_____

_____

my age?_____

_____

my family?_____

_____

my sex?_____

_____

my nationality?_____

_____

my face?_____

_____

What form would these changes take?_____

_____

If I changed a part, how would that affect the whole?_____

_____

Aspects of myself that...

I offer to others_____

_____

I keep for myself_____

_____

remain a mystery to me_____

_____

I am most apt to disown_____

_____

I am most pleased with_____

_____

seem to have a life of their own_____

_____

come through strongly_____

_____

seldom fail me_____

_____

appear outside my control_____

_____

surprise me with their force_____

_____

are humbling_____

_____

I could never deny_____

_____

Possessions that...

are precious to me_____

_____

remind me of who I am_____

_____

remind me of who I love_____

_____

18 | Possessions that...

remind me of where I've been_____

_____

have been misplaced_____

_____

have been broken_____

_____

have been sold_____

_____

have been given away_____

_____

have outlived their usefulness_____

_____

are of lasting value_____

_____

I am grateful for_____

_____

What in my life would I like to cut away?_____

_____

What can I do without?_____

_____

What can I recycle or transform?_____

_____

What can I breathe new life into?_____

_____

What can I give away?_____

_____

What will be my legacy or inheritance?_____

_____

Who do I bequeath my worldly goods and wisdom to?_____

_____

Whose lot has been cast with mine?_____

_____

I was born into the religious tradition of_____

_____

What do I appreciate about my religious training?_____

_____

What would I change?_____

_____

How did I express my spirituality as a child?_____

_____

What was the response from those around me?_____

_____

Who or what sent me in a spiritual direction?_____

_____

Where did I go with it?_____

_____

I once thought that God_____

_____

20 | I once thought that God...

I now believe_____

_____

I have a deep faith in_____

_____

I practice what I believe by_____

_____

I have a sense of the sacred in my life whenever_____

_____

To explain what I mean by sacred, I would use these words___

_____

To define what is profane, I would say_____

_____

A sacred place I have been is_____

_____

A holy person I know_____

_____

I have been blessed with_____

_____

I felt "the hand of God" when_____

_____

What does it mean to live a spiritual life?_____

_____

Who do I know that has lived a life of devotion?_____

_____

I would describe this experience as mystical_____

_____

What is my idea of eternity?_____

_____

What are my secret meditations? Prayers?_____

_____

What is the sacred obligation I have been entrusted with?_____

_____

Heroes and heroines I have met...

in books_____

_____

on television_____

_____

in the movies_____

_____

who are athletes_____

_____

who are public figures_____

_____

who are artists_____

_____

who are musicians_____

_____

22 | Why are they great?_____

_____

What are their flaws?_____

_____

What are the pivotal points in their life stories?_____

_____

In my memorable dreams_____

_____

What are the settings for these dreams?_____

_____

What am I trying to do?_____

_____

What are the elements or symbols in my dreams?_____

_____

What do they mean in my family?_____

_____

Where are they found in paintings or in movies?_____

_____

What are their dictionary definitions?_____

_____

What do they mean to me?_____

_____

Are there universal meanings?_____

_____

Who repeatedly appears in my dreams?_____

_____

What do I keep running away from?_____

_____

What dreams did I want to continue?_____

_____

What dreams caused me to wake up terrified?_____

_____

What dreams caused me to wake up laughing?_____

_____

As a child, I dreamt_____

_____

My parent told me of a dream where_____

_____

I was told I appeared in another person's dream, where I_____

_____

In my recurring daydreams, I see myself...

wearing_____

_____

spending time with_____

_____

owning_____

_____

24 | In my recurring daydreams, I see myself...

saying_____

_____

helping_____

_____

living_____

_____

acting as if_____

_____

making_____

_____

knowing_____

_____

Other thoughts...

2
My Body

I have said that the soul is
not more than the body,
And I have said that the body
is not more than the soul,
And nothing, not God, is
greater to one and than one's
self is.

Walt Whitman
Song of Myself

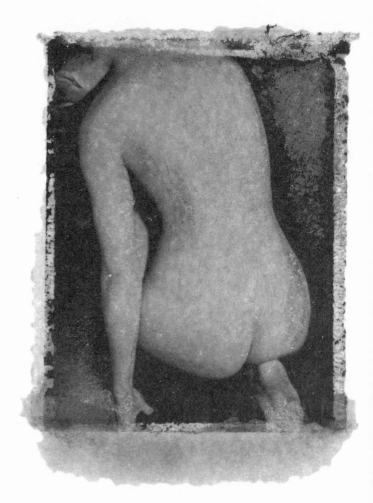

A physical description of myself as a child would be_____

_____

What was it like to be a child in my body?_____

_____

What has my body taught me as I get older?_____

_____

I would describe the color and shape of my eyes as_____

_____

I would describe my skin as_____

_____

I would describe the texture of my hair as_____

_____

Which of my senses is the strongest? How do I know?_____

_____

What do I enjoy about being my...

    body type?_____

_____

    height?_____

_____

    sex?_____

_____

    color?_____

_____

30 | When do I feel comfortable in my own skin?_____

_____

Is there someone I love who resembles me?_____

_____

Have I ever seen a face in a work of art or photograph that is similar to mine?_____

_____

It was a revelation to discover that my body_____

_____

When have I neglected my body?_____

_____

When have I taken good care of my body?_____

_____

What are my favorite photographs of myself?_____

    What are my favorite photographs from my childhood?_____

    _____

    When I look at these photographs I realize_____

    _____

    Who else is in the photos?_____

    _____

    Who were the photographers?_____

    _____

    Why were they taken?_____

    _____

    What happened before and after the photos were taken?_____

    _____

Where are these photos now?_____

_____

Who would I like to make a portrait of me?_____

_____

What should be in the background?_____

_____

What is my best feature?_____

_____

When have I felt graceful?_____

_____

When have I felt powerful?_____

_____

Who has been critical of my body?_____

_____

How do I treat my body with respect?_____

_____

Where on my body do I carry scars?_____

_____

Where in the body do I feel...

joy?_____

_____

sadness?_____

_____

apprehension?_____

_____

32 | Where in the body do I feel...

certainty?_____

_____

I usually feel robust when_____

_____

I tend to become ill when_____

_____

I generally feel weary when_____

_____

I know my own strength when_____

_____

If I had been born the opposite sex...

What would my life be like?_____

_____

What choices would I have made differently?_____

_____

What would I have suppressed?_____

_____

Which character traits would remain the same?_____

_____

Who of my own sex do I emulate?_____

_____

What do they know that I want to know?_____

_____

When have I felt neither male nor female? _____

_____

These are the men and women who informed my views about...

women's bodies _____

_____

men's bodies _____

_____

sexuality _____

_____

physical prowess _____

_____

beauty _____

_____

What did they believe? _____

_____

I never had the stomach for _____

_____

My heart soared when _____

_____

I got my back up when _____

_____

I wish I had the nerve to _____

_____

34 I had a hand in_____

_____

I have an eye for_____

_____

What are my body's...

pleasures?_____

_____

pains?_____

_____

limitations?_____

_____

powers?_____

_____

When do I make myself...

decorative?_____

_____

plain?_____

_____

When do I have fits of energy?_____

_____

When am I inhibited?_____

_____

When my body is in motion, I_____

_____

My sleeping patterns tend to be_____

_____

What has been the balance of health and illness throughout my life?_____

_____

When have I feared for...

my health?_____

_____

my life?_____

_____

These were the childhood illnesses I suffered_____

_____

What minor illnesses have I known?_____

_____

How did they affect my spirit?_____

_____

When was I gravely ill?_____

_____

Where did I go to recover?_____

_____

Who was there for me?_____

_____

What sensations did I observe?_____

_____

How did I recover?_____

_____

36 | To heal myself, I_____

_____

What parts of me have been healed?_____

_____

To improve my health, I_____

_____

What is on the mend?_____

_____

What may never get better?_____

_____

A sudden change in my health was brought about by_____

_____

As time progresses, my thoughts about my body have changed from_____

_____

to_____

I sensed a raw strength within_____

_____

I saw an unexpected beauty in myself when_____

_____

When my beloved sees me, I am_____

_____

My body knows more than my mind about_____

_____

My mind knows more than my body when it comes to_____

_____

What answers lie in the body alone?_____

_____

If the body doesn't lie, mine is trying to say_____

_____

I was humbled by my body when_____

_____

My body has served me well by_____

_____

My body seems to contradict my spirit by_____

_____

These are the nonphysical traits my body expresses_____

_____

38 | *Other thoughts...*

3 Myself With Others

The way you wear your hat,
The way you sip your tea,
The mem'ry of all that,
No, no, they can't take that
away from me...

George and Ira Gershwin
"They Can't Take That
Away From Me"

Who is most like me?_____

_____

How am I unlike anyone else?_____

_____

Who do I aspire to be like?_____

_____

Who would I like to meet again?_____

_____

Who would I like to thank?_____

_____

Who have been my teachers?_____

_____

Who delivered a vital message?_____

_____

Who raised me?_____

_____

Who did I wish were my parents?_____

_____

Who is like a sister or a brother?_____

_____

Who is like a long-lost twin?_____

_____

42 | Who has ignored me?_____

_____

Who did I need to protect myself from?_____

_____

Who surprised and pleased me with their friendship?_____

_____

Who was I afraid to get to know?_____

_____

Who is waiting to hear from me?_____

_____

Who has waited for me?_____

_____

Who wrote to me when I was far from home?_____

_____

Who would brave the elements to look for me?_____

_____

Who came to see me when I was ill?_____

_____

Who came to see me when I was in trouble?_____

_____

Who makes me laugh in spite of everything?_____

_____

Who enjoys my company?_____

_____

Who do I confide in?_____

_____

Who do I like to see every so often?_____

_____

Who should I steer clear of?_____

_____

Who do I like to meet for coffee?_____

_____

Who do I like to walk with?_____

_____

Who do I enjoy talking with on the phone?_____

_____

Who would I choose to stand beside always?_____

_____

Of those I have known, who is the most...

    desirable?_____

_____

    enigmatic?_____

_____

    forthright?_____

_____

    kind?_____

_____

44 | Of those I have known, who is the most...

gifted?_____

_____

resourceful?_____

_____

melancholic?_____

_____

dramatic?_____

_____

original?_____

_____

saintly?_____

_____

fortunate?_____

_____

tragic?_____

_____

otherworldly?_____

_____

gentle?_____

_____

imaginative?_____

_____

courageous?_____

_____

annoying?_____

_____

musical?_____

_____

witty?_____

_____

knowledgeable?_____

_____

graceful?_____

_____

reliable?_____

_____

noble?_____

_____

genuine?_____

_____

I will always feel indebted to_____

_____

Someone who turned my head was_____

_____

I could always breathe easier around_____

_____

46 | I often wonder what happened to_____

_____

I am sorry I lost touch with_____

_____

I was once close to_____ but now_____

_____

I may never see_____ again, but they changed my life for the better

because_____

My friendship with_____ has run its course because_____

_____

My friendship with_____is still pleasurable because_____

_____

Which friendships belong to a specific time and place?_____

_____

Which friendships have endured?_____

_____

Who can I see only every so often and still pick up where we left off?_____

_____

Which friendships were unexpected?_____

_____

Who are the influential women in my life?_____

_____

What are their outstanding attributes?_____

_____

What have they taught me about myself?_____

_____

Who are the influential men in my life?_____

_____

What are their outstanding character traits?_____

_____

How do I feel when I am around them?_____

_____

What did my parents say about...

their life together?_____

_____

raising children?_____

_____

men and women?_____

_____

their race?_____

_____

work?_____

_____

their nationality?_____

_____

48 | What did my parents say about...

God?_____

_____

sex?_____

_____

my birth and infancy?_____

_____

Who are my favorite relations?_____

_____

Who are the wise ones in my family?_____

_____

Who does my family say I take after?_____

_____

At family gatherings, who is the "head of the family"?_____

_____

Who knows and keeps the family history?_____

_____

Who are the feared relations?_____

_____

Who knows the family secrets?_____

_____

These are the stories I would tell my children_____

_____

Although not born to me, this young person could be my child_____

_____

What should a father say to a daughter?_____

_____

What should a mother say to a son?_____

_____

These are the family stories that...

    feature my parents as children_____

_____

    tell me how my parents met_____

_____

    tell me about my grandparents, cousins_____

_____

    reveal the nature of my relationship with my siblings_____

_____

    describe an action of mine_____

_____

    explain why my parents married_____

_____

    are told in a language other than English_____

_____

    are about people I've never met_____

_____

    reveal the hopes and fears of my ancestors_____

_____

    indicate the unwritten rules within my family_____

_____

50 | These are the family stories that...

tell me what is sacred to my family_____

_____

In the novel that could be written about my family, we...

always_____

_____

would never_____

_____

still_____

_____

should have known_____

_____

loved_____

_____

labored_____

_____

laughed at_____

_____

believed in_____

_____

always knew_____

_____

were afraid_____

lost_____

hoped for_____

took for granted_____

prayed for_____

catered to_____

had plenty of_____

lost_____

broke_____

overlooked_____

left behind_____

arrived_____

52 | In the novel that could be written about my family, we...

grew_____

_____

ate_____

_____

settled_____

_____

never spoke of_____

_____

visited_____

_____

were separated_____

_____

celebrated_____

_____

found_____

_____

slept_____

_____

neglected_____

_____

relied upon_____

_____

admired_____

_____

inherited_____

_____

What are the gaps in my family history?_____

_____

What part of me has remained "home" with my family?_____

_____

What part has moved on?_____

_____

What piece of home do I carry with me?_____

_____

I feel part of my family when_____

_____

I was proud to be a member of my family when_____

_____

Children have taught me_____

_____

I believe I taught my parents_____

_____

I would like my family to know_____

_____

I would like my friends to remember_____

_____

I would like my beloved to please me soon by_____

_____

54 | I cannot deny my feelings of...

love for_____

_____

respect for_____

_____

longing for_____

_____

fondness for_____

_____

suspicion of_____

_____

envy of_____

_____

being in awe of_____

_____

Who is my heart's true desire?_____

_____

How do I know?_____

_____

At what moment did I realize this person was for me?_____

_____

What is the truth that exists between us?_____

_____

What do we recognize in each other? _____

_____

I have always believed that love _____

_____

I now know that love _____

_____

I never understood why my love life _____

_____

In my love life, I would love to _____

_____

In my love life, I would prefer not to _____

_____

It was a pleasure to love _____

_____

I felt desired when _____

_____

I wanted to but never kissed _____

_____

For a brief time, I loved _____

_____

My first love was _____

_____

My eleventh-hour love was _____

_____

56 | To be happy in love, what sort of care and attention do I require?_____

_____

I recognized my sexual self when_____

_____

What has been my deepest experience of love?_____

_____

Why should I keep my heart open?_____

_____

Who was my first crush?_____

_____

When was my first kiss?_____

_____

When was my love unrequited?_____

_____

I let love slip through my fingers when_____

_____

Like ships passing in the night, we loved_____

_____

Who was my most recent crush?_____

_____

Who will I always long for?_____

_____

When have I found myself in a love triangle?_____

_____

Who backed away?_____

_____

In my love life, I courted disaster when_____

_____

When did I talk myself out of love?_____

_____

Whose love was I unable to return?_____

_____

My love went unnoticed when_____

_____

When I think of the ones I loved and lost, I wonder_____

_____

What would I say if I were to see them today?_____

_____

What were our best times?_____

_____

What was our worst day?_____

_____

What would I return to them?_____

_____

What can I thank them for?_____

_____

58 | What questions would I ask them?_____

_____

Gifts I received that were...

handmade_____

_____

edible_____

_____

financial_____

_____

spoken_____

_____

of practical assistance_____

_____

of encouragement_____

_____

of acknowledgement_____

_____

extravagant_____

_____

animal, vegetable or mineral_____

_____

heirlooms_____

_____

What alliances have I carefully established and sustained?_____

_____

With respect to social responsibilities, who shares my values?_____

_____

Who have been my counselors and advisors...

    as a young adult?_____

    _____

    in the recent past?_____

    _____

How did they guide me?_____

_____

What did they say?_____

_____

What did they convey?_____

_____

Someone who taught me to respect myself_____

_____

Someone who helped me know myself_____

_____

Whose...

    opinions have I considered?_____

    _____

    respect do I desire?_____

    _____

    understanding do I rely upon?_____

    _____

60 | Whose...

advice do I seek?_____

_____

Where do my counselors go for counseling?_____

_____

Who has the same strengths as I?_____

_____

Who will never understand me?_____

_____

What do I often hear myself say when I am critical of others?_____

_____

Who has been a stranger to me?_____

_____

What is the unrealized potential I see in someone I love dearly?_____

_____

What is the quality and temperament I value most in a companion?_____

_____

Which relationship has been the most...

challenging?_____

_____

solid?_____

_____

uplifting?_____

_____

purest?_____

_____

troubled?_____

_____

mysterious?_____

_____

blessed?_____

_____

oppressive?_____

_____

incorruptible?_____

_____

Who have been my adversaries?_____

_____

How have they been worthy adversaries?_____

_____

Why do they oppose me?_____

_____

What do I love and loathe about them?_____

_____

Who would I invite to celebrate my good fortune?_____

_____

Who judges me harshly?_____

_____

62 | Who has helped me face the world?_____

_____

Who makes time stand still?_____

_____

Who would know me anywhere?_____

_____

I keep meeting women who_____

_____

I keep meeting men who_____

_____

These are the types of people who are drawn to me_____

_____

Now I know how to attract_____

_____

Now I know how to avoid_____

_____

People I would like to...

    spend more time with_____

_____

    lend my support to_____

_____

People I...

    trust implicitly_____

_____

could never appreciate_____

_____

thank God for_____

_____

generally agree with_____

_____

find calming_____

_____

always laugh with_____

_____

know appreciate me_____

_____

I'll never forget...

the sight of_____ dancing with_____

_____

the night we sang_____

_____

how_____ saved the day when_____

_____

The highest way to honor the presence of...

a friend_____

_____

my beloved_____

_____

64 | The highest way to honor the presence of...

a parent_____

_____

a child_____

_____

Other thoughts...

4
Myself Alone

Solitude, my mother,
tell me my life again.

Oscar de la Milosz

These habits or routine activities...

give me great pleasure_____

_____

offer me peace of mind_____

_____

stimulate me_____

_____

Keepsakes that I carry with me_____

_____

I feel at home wherever there is_____

_____

For me, the key to happiness has always been_____

_____

What do I require for survival?_____

_____

These are the superficial things I insist upon_____

_____

What are the luxuries I crave?_____

_____

Where do I seek...

peace?_____

_____

pleasure?_____

_____

68 | Where do I seek...

freedom?_____

_____

What are the best times of the day for me?_____

_____

I feel most comfortable during this season_____

_____

The best foods are_____

_____

The best weather is_____

_____

I feel refreshed when_____

_____

When do I have surges of energy?_____

_____

When do I feel weighted down?_____

_____

What makes me irritable?_____

_____

What keeps me up nights?_____

_____

What gets me out of bed in the morning?_____

_____

When do I allow curiosity to be my guide?_____

_____

What am I curious about?_____

_____

What is the first section of the newspaper that I read?_____

_____

Which sections go untouched?_____

_____

What were my best ideas?_____

_____

When did I turn out to be right after all?_____

_____

What ideas were best left unrealized?_____

_____

Where has my creativity led me?_____

_____

How do I accomplish things in the world?_____

_____

I am drawn to these...

languages_____

_____

landscapes_____

_____

periods in history_____

_____

schools of thought_____

_____

70 | I am drawn to these...

styles of music_____

_____

periods of art_____

_____

These are the books...

I read more than once_____

_____

I loved as a child_____

_____

that opened my eyes as a young person_____

_____

Music I have...

listened to over and over_____

_____

danced to_____

_____

heard performed live_____

_____

been introduced to by a friend_____

_____

been introduced to by my parents_____

_____

Beloved...

fairy tales and children's stories_____

_____

passages from scripture_____

_____

movies_____

_____

television shows_____

_____

stories I heard through the grapevine_____

_____

stories of athletic feats_____

_____

comedies_____

_____

poems_____

_____

Beloved novels...

Who are the main characters?_____

_____

What do they aspire to?_____

_____

What do they need?_____

_____

72 | The main characters in beloved novels...

Who helps them?_____

_____

What stands in their way?_____

_____

What are their strengths and weaknesses?_____

_____

What becomes of them?_____

_____

Why are they of interest to me?_____

_____

When it comes to books, I prefer_____ to_____

_____

When it comes to music, I prefer_____ to_____

_____

When it comes to men, I prefer_____ to_____

_____

When it comes to women, I prefer_____ to_____

_____

When it comes to friendship, I prefer_____ to_____

_____

When it comes to cities, I prefer_____to_____

_____

If I was spun around to the point of disorientation, I would instinctively head to...

bed because_____

_____

the doctor because_____

_____

the airport because_____

_____

the library because_____

_____

the mall because_____

_____

the refrigerator because_____

_____

work because_____

_____

a friend because_____

_____

the hills because_____

_____

the arms of_____ because_____

_____

a bar because_____

_____

74 | If I was spun around to the point of disorientation, I would instinctively head to...

the movies because_____

_____

a bookstore because_____

_____

the woods because_____

_____

the gym because_____

_____

a temple or church because_____

_____

the beach because_____

_____

the door because_____

_____

the drawing board because_____

_____

hell and back because_____

_____

Then where would I go?_____

_____

When I come home to an empty house, what is the first thing I do?_____

_____

What do I say when I'm talking to myself?_____

_____

Where would I never be seen?_____

_____

What is my secret destination?_____

_____

Who waits for me there?_____

_____

What are my private ambitions?_____

_____

Why can they never be realized?_____

_____

Why should I try?_____

_____

What will I always know how to do?_____

_____

I can safely say, "I will never ever_____

_____

I accepted my limitations when_____

_____

I now know I cannot_____

_____

I insist that I will not_____

_____

I neglected my responsibilities when_____

_____

76 | To this day, I regret_____

_____

I often have misgivings about_____

_____

When I trace my thoughts, where do my worries begin?_____

_____

What are my pressing concerns?_____

_____

What do I judge myself harshly about?_____

_____

To give myself peace of mind, what could be...

clarified?_____

_____

spoken?_____

_____

acknowledged?_____

_____

edged?_____

_____

finished?_____

_____

begun?_____

_____

When did I make the best of a bad bargain?_____

_____

When have I been resourceful in adverse circumstances?_____

_____

I kidded myself when_____

_____

What were the uses of that self-deception?_____

_____

I lied to someone when_____

_____

Why didn't I tell the truth?_____

_____

What secrets have I been able to keep?_____

_____

What is the biggest secret of my life so far?_____

_____

When have my imagination and intention...

provided a reprieve from suffering?_____

_____

created a misunderstanding?_____

_____

found a solution when none seemed possible?_____

_____

helped me to negotiate a way through this world?_____

_____

enabled me to forge an identity I could live with?_____

_____

78 | Which observations have I made in a state of...

happiness?_____

_____

distraction?_____

_____

panic?_____

_____

anguish?_____

_____

grace?_____

_____

What emotions do I feel most often?_____

_____

What is numb?_____

_____

What saps my strength?_____

_____

When have I been bored to tears?_____

_____

How do my difficult moods pass?_____

_____

What does my joy tell me?_____

_____

What does my sorrow tell me?_____

_____

I am grateful for_____

_____

I once wanted_____

_____

I now miss_____

_____

I am glad I never_____

_____

I always save_____

_____

No one knows that I_____

_____

No one knows that I want_____

_____

I knew I was alone when_____

_____

I felt understood when_____

_____

I felt appreciated when_____

_____

I was seen for my true colors when_____

_____

80 | I saw myself in a different light when_____

_____

It took me awhile, but I now understand the significance of_____

_____

It never ceases to amaze me that I_____

_____

When did someone else's happiness move me?_____

_____

When did someone else's grief move me?_____

_____

When have I known my own heart?_____

_____

Have I ever had an experience of "waking up" to the truth?_____

_____

What choices did I make then?_____

_____

When did I know something had come to a close?_____

_____

How did I make an experience "my own"?_____

_____

When have I changed for the better?_____

_____

What initial step did I take?_____

_____

How do I prepare for change?_____

_____

When am I...

nervous?_____

_____

at ease?_____

_____

How do I handle embarrassment?_____

_____

What is my fatal flaw?_____

_____

How is it a virtue?_____

_____

What do I have a gift for?_____

_____

How is it a burden?_____

_____

I know I have accomplished_____

_____

I know that I don't know_____

_____

All along I have known_____

_____

82 | *Other thoughts...*

5 *Myself in Time*

honor the past but
welcome the future
(and dance your death
away at this wedding)
never mind the world with
its' heroes and villains
for god likes girls and
tomorrow and the earth

e.e. cummings
"dive for dreams"

I will always have time for _____

_____

Time well-spent is _____

_____

When has it seemed like time was standing still? _____

_____

When has time flown? _____

_____

Is there a time in my life I would return to? _____

_____

I came of age in this time and place _____

_____

What are the characteristic vices and virtues of my time? _____

_____

How do I mark time? _____

_____

Which dates do I remember easily? _____

_____

Every week I _____

_____

Every month I _____

_____

Every decade I _____

_____

86 | I am most fully in the present when_____

_____

In those moments, I remember_____

_____

I forget_____

_____

These are the milestones I have measured my life by_____

_____

I knew I had matured when_____

_____

I feel young again when_____

_____

There was no time like the time_____

_____

Times of triumph when I realized...

life could be good_____

_____

I could trust myself_____

_____

I could trust other people_____

_____

I possessed what I truly needed_____

_____

I created something previously undreamed of_____

_____

I could live in accord with my values_____

_____

Trying times when I was...

without_____

_____

a stranger to myself_____

_____

Times I...

felt part of a whole_____

_____

was drawn into a circle_____

_____

stumbled into friendly territory_____

_____

If I arrange my life into seven-year periods...

What were my hopes and fears?_____

_____

Who was most important to me?_____

_____

What was my relationship to the natural world?_____

_____

How did I feel about where I was living?_____

_____

What was I hoping to accomplish?_____

_____

88 | If I arrange my life into seven-year periods...

What was outside my control?_____

_____

What do I carry with me today from that time?_____

_____

Why am I glad that time is over?_____

_____

What could I do all over again?_____

_____

I celebrated the birth(s) of_____ by_____

_____

I celebrated the marriage(s) of_____ by_____

_____

What is the least meaningful religious or secular holiday for me?_____

_____

How do I avoid participating in it?_____

_____

What is the most meaningful religious or secular holiday for me?_____

_____

How can it best be celebrated?_____

_____

What is the joy in it for me?_____

_____

What is the mystery in it for me?_____

_____

These ceremonies have marked the phases of my life_____

_____

How did the ceremony compare with what I was feeling?_____

_____

Who prepared me for the event?_____

_____

How did my life change?_____

_____

What was my first experience of death?_____

_____

Who told me about this and other significant deaths?_____

_____

Who did I tell?_____

_____

Who did I turn to for comfort?_____

_____

How did we honor the deceased?_____

_____

Hard times when I felt...

lost_____

_____

awkward _____

_____

put-upon_____

_____

90 | Hard times when I felt...

in pain_____

_____

bereft_____

_____

misunderstood_____

_____

oppressed_____

_____

estranged from others_____

_____

When did I first know I was in trouble?_____

_____

Who else knew?_____

_____

How did I try to solve it?_____

_____

What do I know now that I did not know then?_____

_____

Could this have been avoided?_____

_____

What was the sequence of events that led to it?_____

_____

When did I come to understand the significance of these events?_____

_____

What truths did I find at the center of this ordeal?_____

_____

What is the humor in it?_____

_____

What habits, for better or for worse, did I practice during this time?_____

_____

How did my social life change during this time?_____

_____

How did my work life change during this time?_____

_____

What was of greatest concern to me?_____

_____

What did I learn?_____

_____

What was I able to accomplish or express?_____

_____

When did I tell the whole truth about it?_____

_____

Who was able to hear it?_____

_____

How can I transform it into something I want to carry with me?_____

_____

92 | A time in my life that shaped me_____

_____

I would describe myself at that time as_____

_____

A striking image from that time is_____

_____

The music that recalls that time_____

_____

The people who made that time what it was_____

_____

The books I was reading then_____

_____

One memorable conversation at that time was_____

_____

I will never forget that during that time_____

_____

A habit I practiced then was_____

_____

At that time, I thoroughly enjoyed_____

_____

One unexpected turn of events was_____

_____

A skill I acquired at that time_____

_____

World events I can recall_____

_____

I was coming from_____ and then heading toward_____

_____

My present circumstances could best be described as_____

_____

This time in my life helps me to understand which times in my life more clearly?_____

_____

What do I long to understand about my history?_____

_____

Who can help me understand?_____

_____

What would I like to put to rest?_____

_____

If happiness in the present is the best plan for the future, what am I doing to be happy

now?_____

_____

94 | *Other thoughts...*

6 Myself in the World

My joy, my grief, my
hope, my love, did all
within this circle move.

Edmund Waller
On a Girdle

Places...

I have returned to _____

_____

I diligently cared for _____

_____

that reappear in my dreams at night _____

_____

I return to in my dreams by day _____

_____

where I felt lost _____

_____

that I claimed for myself _____

_____

that are strange, but familiar _____

_____

that never felt like home _____

_____

How do I get my bearings...

at family gatherings? _____

_____

in a meeting? _____

_____

in a new city? _____

_____

98 | How do I get my bearings...

    in a museum?_____

    _____

    in the woods?_____

    _____

    on a train?_____

    _____

    at a party?_____

    _____

    in a foreign country?_____

    _____

Places...

    that changed me forever_____

    _____

    I go to find solace_____

    _____

    I go to get inspired_____

    _____

Memorable places, near and far, that I found...

    ancient_____

    _____

    neglected_____

    _____

dangerous_____

_____

holy_____

_____

empty_____

_____

tragic_____

_____

romantic_____

_____

Was I alone there?_____

_____

How did I get there?_____

_____

In my first job, I_____

_____

The unpaid work I do is_____

_____

Compared with what I had imagined, my work life is_____

_____

Compared to the working lives of my parents, mine is_____

_____

What is the definition of my work ethic?_____

_____

100 | Whose example taught me my work ethic?_____

_____

This is my vision of an ideal work life_____

_____

Do I feel my work is a vocation?_____

_____

Who does my work serve?_____

_____

What is the evidence for this?_____

_____

What is humane in my work?_____

_____

The best part of my work day is_____

_____

I am enriched by the work I do when_____

_____

Who is my ally at work?_____

_____

Who is my accomplice?_____

_____

Who are the villains?_____

_____

What materials have served me well in my work?_____

_____

What tasks have I now mastered?_____

_____

What do I hope to learn?_____

_____

When am I most confident at work?_____

_____

What do I do that no one else can accomplish?_____

_____

What parts of myself languish in my present work?_____

_____

What opens up a sense of possibility for me?_____

_____

When do I get bogged down?_____

_____

I would describe my work environment as_____

_____

   What keeps me there?_____

_____

   What would prompt me to leave?_____

_____

What is the unspoken aim of my work?_____

_____

This part of my job really means the most to me_____

_____

102 | What talents do I truly possess?_____

_____

What ability am I known for?_____

_____

Why do others come to me?_____

_____

What are the needs that match my talents?_____

_____

How much money is enough for a yearly salary?_____

_____

What would I do with a windfall?_____

_____

How much money is too much?_____

_____

Money came to me when I needed it when_____

_____

I am indebted to_____

_____

My money was well-spent when I_____

_____

I wasted money when_____

_____

I know I can now do without_____

_____

I should put money aside for_____

_____

Who can help me manage my money?_____

_____

I have always had plenty of_____

_____

I should contribute to_____

_____

I earned what I deserved when_____

_____

I was the recipient of charity when_____

_____

I practiced charity when_____

_____

I got a financial reprieve when_____

_____

I feel enriched whenever_____

_____

What do I need to feel beyond want?_____

_____

I saw justice prevail when_____

_____

I witnessed injustice when_____

_____

104 | These are the moral questions that...

I have witnessed_____

_____

appear just outside my front door_____

_____

speak to me from the past_____

_____

involve me directly_____

_____

shaped my early life_____

_____

influence the young people I care about_____

_____

are clearer to me now_____

_____

The obligations I pass on to others are_____

_____

I am responsible for_____

_____

I committed a sin of omission when_____

_____

These are the acts of heroism that I have witnessed_____

_____

These are the acts of heroism that I have committed_____

_____

In my world, I have observed many things, and this...

I don't yet understand_____

_____

no one talks about_____

_____

I would like to write about_____

_____

106 | *Other thoughts...*

7
Myself in Nature

Two or three hours
walking will carry me
to as strange a country
as ever I expect to see

Henry David Thoreau
Walking

In my everyday life, I experience the natural world through_____

_____

I come alive when the weather is_____

_____

My favorite time of day is_____

_____

If I could, everyday I would walk to_____

_____

What draws me into the natural world?_____

_____

What am I looking for?_____

_____

I recognize these types of...

flowers_____

_____

trees_____

_____

birds_____

_____

rocks_____

_____

The strangest landscape I have seen was_____

_____

110 | The place closest to wilderness I have known_____

_____

An almost uninhabited place I visited_____

_____

An unspoiled country I have seen_____

_____

The most beautiful garden I have seen_____

_____

The strangest garden I have seen_____

_____

The most magnificent animals I have seen_____

_____

Where and when have I seen them?_____

_____

What observations have I made in the natural world?_____

_____

What has recently changed in my natural surroundings?_____

_____

I first observed the power of nature when_____

_____

Since then I have noticed_____

_____

I was at the mercy of nature when_____

_____

I was exposed to the elements when_____

_____

   And I learned that_____

_____

In the natural world, I fear_____

_____

How do I protect myself from the malevolent forces of nature?_____

_____

What body of water do I often visit?_____

_____

What times of the year do I go there?_____

_____

Do I prefer lakes, rivers, the ocean or springs?_____

_____

What bodies of water do I like to swim in?_____

_____

What bodies of water do I like to wade in?_____

_____

Which forests and woods are closest to me?_____

_____

Which forests and woods were closest to where I lived as a child?_____

_____

The highest altitude I have experienced is_____

_____

What did I observe there?_____

_____

What do I first notice at the change of each season?_____

_____

What is the furthest from home I have traveled...

    north?_____

_____

    south?_____

_____

    east?_____

_____

    west?_____

_____

I am most familiar with this...

    mountain range_____

_____

    beach_____

_____

    field_____

_____

    stretch of road_____

_____

If I have lived on an island, how has that affected me?_____

_____

If I haven't lived on an island, which would I choose?_____

_____

What is the driest place I have been?_____

_____

What colors did I see there?_____

_____

What could I smell?_____

_____

Animals that came into my life that...

I rescued_____

_____

were a nuisance_____

_____

were a treasure_____

_____

were a menace_____

_____

became my companions_____

_____

Who named them?_____

_____

I can recall these...

strange weather conditions_____

_____

114 | I can recall these...

natural disasters_____

_____

beautiful freaks of nature_____

_____

fantastic storms_____

_____

seasonal maladies_____

_____

solar and lunar eclipses_____

_____

visible constellations_____

_____

What phases of my life match the characteristics of...

winter, if winter means *solitude, austerity, rectification, darkness, silence, resolve, depth, faith, patience, preparation?*_____

_____

spring, if spring means *renewal, new endeavors, attraction, anticipation, education, curiosity, joy?*_____

_____

summer, if summer means *clarity, vitality, comfort, freedom, pleasure, travel, power, plenty?*_____

_____

autumn, if autumn means *completion, wisdom, teaching, gathering,*

*understanding, community, mastery?*_____

_____

When have I passed from one period to the next?_____

_____

When did the shifts occur?_____

_____

Which season describes my life as I now live it?_____

_____

I strain to hear the sounds of_____

_____

I would love to see a photograph of_____

_____

I would love to see the sight of_____

_____

I would love to see_____ one more time because_____

_____

Often I crave the taste of_____

_____

The smell of_____ recalls this time in my life_____

_____

I would always like to touch_____

_____

116 | For as long as I can remember, I have been pleased by...

the color of_____

_____

shades of_____

_____

the texture of_____

_____

the arrangement of_____

_____

I was once moved by the sight of_____

_____

I was once moved by the sound of_____

_____

I am attuned to the tone of_____

_____

I would go out of my way to...

see_____

_____

hear_____

_____

touch_____

_____

taste_____

_____

smell_____

_____

I long to hear the voice of_____

_____

I once lingered to take in a view of_____

_____

I remember tasting, seeing, touching, smelling, hearing and sensing these things...

in my childhood home_____

_____

at my school_____

_____

in my early travels_____

_____

in my work life_____

_____

Where have I found fertile ground?_____

_____

What substances do I find...

therapeutic?_____

_____

comforting?_____

_____

intolerable?_____

_____

118 | What substances do I find...

stimulating?_____

_____

Which of the elements and conditions do I seek...

fire and intensity?_____

_____

air and transformation?_____

_____

water and intuition?_____

_____

earth and stability?_____

_____

Do I instinctively head north, south, east or west?_____

_____

What do I hope to avoid?_____

_____

What do I expect to find?_____

_____

These are my responsibilities to my environment_____

_____

Other thoughts...

8
My Life Course

Far from planning to
come here, I meant to
sail straight home.

Homer
The Odyssey

My schooling took place in_____

_____

My best teachers were_____

_____

I am thankful to have learned_____

_____

My education is unfinished in the field of_____

_____

My education was determined by_____

_____

I was a reluctant student in the subject of_____

_____

I was a natural student in these subjects_____

_____

I wish I was taught_____

_____

I should have been encouraged to_____

_____

What can never be taught?_____

_____

This is the achievement I take greatest pride in_____

When did I start on that road?_____

_____

How long did it take?_____

_____

When have I withdrawn from the demands of the outside world...

to chart my course?_____

_____

to experience my private sorrows?_____

_____

to experience moments of joy?_____

_____

I followed my heart when_____

_____

I stood my ground when_____

_____

I obeyed the dictates of my conscience when_____

_____

My honesty was tested when_____

_____

I listened to my intuition when_____

_____

Chance encounters when I...

shared my thoughts with a stranger_____

_____

allowed myself a sudden change of plans_____

_____

had a stroke of luck_____

_____

followed a gut feeling_____

_____

found my way as if by accident_____

_____

In my life, these were...

good fortunes and blessings_____

_____

coincidences_____

_____

happy accidents_____

_____

windfalls_____

_____

chance beneficial meetings_____

_____

It was a stroke of luck that_____

_____

In my daily life, it is extraordinary that_____

_____

My life becomes my own when_____

_____

126 | I saw a fork in the road when_____

_____

I made a narrow escape when_____

_____

I catch myself imagining other lives when_____

_____

I recognized the presence of forces in my life beyond my control when_____

_____

A moment of truth was_____

_____

I glimpsed my destiny when_____

_____

I went for broke when_____

_____

I took back my life from the clutches of_____

_____

I threw caution to the winds the day I_____

_____

I tested the waters as I_____

_____

I caught my stride when_____

_____

I let the current carry me to_____

_____

What are my consistent interests?_____

_____

What are my persistent longings?_____

_____

Who has left my life only to return?_____

_____

What has felt predestined?_____

_____

What pattern has been altered?_____

_____

When did I alter my course?_____

_____

Again and again, I find myself_____

_____

I have never felt free to_____

_____

I can always be relied upon_____

_____

No one ever imagined I could, but then I_____

_____

It never occurred to me to_____ until_____

_____

If I hadn't done_____

    I would not have met_____

_____

who introduced me to_____

_____

who in turn introduced me to_____

_____

who told me about_____

_____

which prompted me to_____

_____

when I learned to_____

_____

where I met_____ who_____

_____

I ask myself_____

_____

What are my odd habits?_____

_____

What I have I become in spite of myself?_____

_____

How is my life different than what I imagined as a young person?_____

_____

What is a life well-lived?_____

_____

On an imagined journey...

Who is my ideal companion?_____

_____

What is my destination? _____

_____

Who did I write to along the way? _____

_____

My travel diary...

I left home today feeling _____

_____

They saw me off and said to me as I was leaving _____

_____

At the airport, I _____

_____

At the train station, I _____

_____

As I arrived, I was thinking _____

_____

I was given directions by _____ who told me this story ___

_____

I spent the night _____

_____

What did I buy there? _____

_____

What did I find to eat there? _____

_____

Where did I stay? _____

_____

I was en route to_____ when_____

_____

Who invited me to their home for a meal?_____

_____

What did we talk about?_____

_____

Why were they interested in me?_____

_____

I saw the most beautiful_____

_____

I felt threatened by_____

_____

I was completely lost when_____

_____

When did I need to stop traveling and rest?_____

_____

Who did I meet while traveling on buses? On boats? On trains?_____

_____

I was delayed when_____ and it was an unexpected pleasure because_____

_____

I finally found a place only to discover it was closed when_____

_____

I've never seen anything quite like_____

_____

The smell of_____ was overwhelming_____

_____

I was awakened by the sound of_____

_____

I opened a window and looked out to see_____

_____

I took a long walk around_____

_____

I was surprised to find_____

_____

I was surrounded by silence when_____

_____

I began to feel ill when_____

_____

I thought we'd never get to_____

_____

I wish I had brought_____ with me_____

_____

I could have stayed forever at_____

_____

I should be heading home because_____

_____

If life is schooling, what have I been taught?_____

_____

132 | What are the lessons learned through...

perseverance?_____

_____

false starts?_____

_____

trial and error?_____

_____

retrospect?_____

_____

devotion to a cause or ideal?_____

_____

tragic events?_____

_____

What habits have I learned?_____

_____

What habits have I unlearned?_____

_____

What skills have I acquired?_____

_____

These are the questions or worries of my youth that I now have the answers to_____

_____

When did I have the time of my life?_____

_____

I would like a fortune-teller to predict_____

_____

When did I feel a tug of conscience?_____

_____

When did I obey its dictates?_____

_____

In spite of my intentions, I...

became_____

_____

was led to_____

_____

stayed on at_____

_____

left abruptly_____

_____

never completed_____

_____

accomplished_____

_____

wanted to_____

_____

I thought I should be_____ but actually am_____

_____

I was unable to_____ but found that I could_____

_____

I may not have succeeded at_____ but have always been able to_____

_____

134 | It never occurred to me that I could_____ until_____

_____

What are my goals?_____

_____

What have I focused on?_____

_____

What gets accomplished seemingly without effort?_____

_____

The best idea I've had_____

_____

The most ill-conceived plan I've had_____

_____

What quality do I still hope to possess?_____

_____

What information comes to me through dreams?_____

_____

I find myself daydreaming about making these changes_____

_____

In order to change, I would have to sacrifice_____

_____

In order to realize change, I would have to accept_____

_____

What have I given up along the way...

to find love?_____

_____

to change for the better?_____

_____

I knew poverty when_____, and it taught me_____

_____

I have known prosperity when_____, and found_____

_____

What are the difficult episodes or events of my life that led to...

a realization?_____

_____

love?_____

_____

compassion for others?_____

_____

standing up for myself and others?_____

_____

having someone stand up for me?_____

_____

meeting good people?_____

_____

moving to a better home or job?_____

_____

an unexpected benefit?_____

_____

When have I made a sustained effort?_____

_____

What were the results?_____

_____

What have I survived?_____

_____

Have I ever been or felt in exile?_____

_____

Where have I migrated from?_____

_____

Where do I find solace?_____

_____

Where do I find renewal in hard times?_____

_____

As a child, where did I go to find peace?_____

_____

As a young adult, where did I go find peace?_____

_____

Is there something I have been suffering from for as long as I can remember?_____

_____

What is the true cause of my suffering?_____

_____

Why does it recur despite my efforts?_____

_____

When will I be out of the woods?_____

_____

Where have I been looking for a way out?_____

_____

Is there another way?_____

_____

What can I take refuge in today?_____

_____

What was a blessing in disguise?_____

_____

When I felt...

uplifted_____

_____

triumphed_____

_____

suppressed_____

_____

lost_____

_____

recovered_____

_____

Things changed for the better when_____

_____

Things took a turn for the worse as_____

_____

I turned a crucial corner when_____

_____

138 | I got a leg up from_____

_____

I exceeded my own expectations_____

_____

I found a place in the sun when_____

_____

What...

    makes me cry?_____

    _____

    causes concern?_____

    _____

    makes me laugh out loud?_____

    _____

    strikes a cord within me?_____

    _____

    causes anguish?_____

    _____

    gives me pleasure?_____

    _____

    do I find absorbing?_____

    _____

I expressed my deepest truth as_____

_____

I stood alone when_____

_____

I went my own way as_____

_____

If I could apologize for_____

_____

If I could confess to_____

_____

When did I witness my own capacity...

    for deceit?_____

_____

    for pettiness?_____

_____

    for intolerance?_____

_____

When have I increased my capacity for...

    patience?_____

_____

    pleasure?_____

_____

    courage?_____

_____

    ingenuity?_____

_____

140 | When have I increased my capacity for...

charity?_____

_____

understanding?_____

_____

Do I believe in fate? Why or why not?_____

_____

The Fates have...

cursed me with_____

_____

blessed me with_____

_____

This story illustrates how the blessings and curses of fate have both frustrated and served

me_____

_____

When I met a...

villain_____

_____

prophet_____

_____

poet_____

_____

gossip_____

_____

siren_____
_____

saint_____
_____

fraud_____
_____

cad_____
_____

adventurer_____
_____

hermit_____
_____

truant_____
_____

penny-pincher_____
_____

social butterfly_____
_____

homebody_____
_____

spendthrift_____
_____

taskmaster_____
_____

When I was a...

villain_____

_____

prophet_____

_____

poet_____

_____

gossip_____

_____

siren_____

_____

saint_____

_____

fraud_____

_____

cad_____

_____

adventurer_____

_____

hermit_____

_____

truant_____

_____

penny-pincher_____

_____

social butterfly_____

_____

homebody_____

_____

spendthrift_____

_____

taskmaster_____

_____

beauty_____

_____

The truth about_____ is_____

_____

No one would believe me if I told them_____

_____

Yes, it was really like that when I said_____

_____

They say I wasn't there, but I remember_____

_____

It was as if I dreamt it, but it really happened_____

_____

I know exactly how it was_____

_____

144 | What truth do I need to pay attention to now?_____

_____

When did I fail to meet the expectations of others?_____

_____

When did I know I could not meet dictates of my society?_____

_____

What was I never able to learn?_____

_____

    Why is this just as well?_____

_____

    Why does this make me feel badly?_____

_____

Where will I never fit in?_____

_____

    How is this a blessing in disguise?_____

_____

    How would I benefit or suffer by fitting in?_____

_____

Something of importance to me that remains unspoken_____

_____

Something that is better left unsaid_____

_____

Who are my peers?_____

_____

What have they chosen?_____

_____

How am I similar?_____

_____

How am I different?_____

_____

What phase of my life should be held up to the light?_____

_____

What remains in the shadows?_____

_____

What has been my downfall?_____

_____

What has been my pride and joy?_____

_____

What is the source of my...

determination?_____

_____

insecurity?_____

_____

vitality?_____

_____

vanity?_____

_____

I knew I wasn't young anymore when_____

_____

I found my maturity through_____

_____

I never felt older than when_____

_____

I feel young again when_____

_____

I have given up on_____

_____

I hope for_____

_____

When did I work through my frustrations toward a new perspective?_____

_____

I found what I was waiting for when_____

_____

When were my prayers answered?_____

_____

When did I entertain angels unawares?_____

_____

What have I had to wait for?_____

_____

How did it finally come to me?_____

_____

What was it like to receive it?_____

_____

What did I do while I was waiting?_____

_____

My destiny is_____

_____

My cherished hope is_____

_____

What have I wished for others?_____

_____

What is my idea of an artful life?_____

_____

What was more difficult than I expected?_____

_____

What has come to me easily?_____

_____

What has life required of me?_____

_____

How has life surprised me?_____

_____

When has life imposed something that interfered with my plans and wishes?_____

_____

What was the immediate outcome?_____

_____

148 | When has life imposed something that interfered with my plans and wishes?

What has been the effect over time?_____

_____

What is my life is offering me now?_____

_____

Other thoughts...